ESSENTIAL ELEMENTS®

GUITAR REPERTOIRE

MYSTERIOSO

10 ORIGINAL SONGS WITH SPOOKY MELODIES AND RIFFS

by Allan Jaffe

T0066096

CD mastering: Katsuhiko Naito

ISBN-13: 978-1-4234-1957-0
ISBN-10: 1-4234-1957-X

HAL•LEONARD® CORPORATION

7777 W. BLUEMOUND RD. P.O. BOX 13819 MILWAUKEE, WI 53213

In Australia Contact:
Hal Leonard Australia Pty. Ltd.
4 Lentara Court
Cheltenham, Victoria, 3192 Australia
Email: ausadmin@halleonard.com.au

Visit Hal Leonard Online at
www.halleonard.com

PREFACE

One of the main problems facing the contemporary non-classical guitar teacher is the lack of repertoire available for the serious guitar student. One can find many method books and books devoted to special techniques or musical styles, but it is difficult to find graded volumes of compositions written for the plectrum guitar. In my childhood studies of piano, violin, and cello, one of the aspects that maintained my interest was the wealth of repertoire books geared toward the beginner. For piano alone one can find such great collections as Schumann's Album for the Young and Scenes from Childhood, Bach's Notebook for Anna Magdalena Bach, and Bartok's Mikrokosmos, any of which can serve as a wonderful model for beginning instrumental study. In these volumes, one finds pieces that develop musicianship and give the student a body of good music to play.

In my work as a guitar teacher, I have often written my own exercises and compositions for my students to fill this gap. Needless to say, it was with great pleasure that I accepted the opportunity to create a book of repertoire for the intermediate guitar student for Hal Leonard. This gave me the chance to collect some of my ideas in a cohesive volume, creating a group of pieces that was both musical and developmental. In addition to this, part of my assignment was to use the theme of mystery and suspense as a unifying concept for these pieces. Considering my childhood fascination with mystery and horror, this was right up my alley.

I had earlier written a guitar piece entitled "Mysterioso." With a bit of developing, this piece not only seemed to fit nicely into the concept, but also offered an apt title for the book. My next step was to come up with nine more titles. It occurred to me that it would help the book conceptually if the titles referred not only to the mystery concept, but also to the particular musical skill, event, or mood that was being addressed by the composition. Thus, in "The Chase," a study in harmonic inversions, the fingers seem to chase up the neck of the guitar. "A Daunting Haunting" uses inversions of A minor along with the harmonic minor scale and a slow triplet feel to create a spooky atmosphere. As suggested by its title, "The Plot Thickens" is additive, starting out as a simple bass line, with each repeat getting more and more dense, ending in a full-blown bass and chordal melody.

In writing these pieces, it was my intention to provide the student with music that was idiomatic to the music of our time. "Guitar Noir" and "The Gumshoe's Smooth Move" both contain chord progressions and melodic patterns one might find in a blues or a rock piece. Many of the rhythms of these compositions will be familiar to most fans of contemporary music. Thus, in learning these pieces, students will be adding to the musical language they may be using in other contexts.

Finally, one of the great challenges of plectrum guitar is that of playing a solo piece that sounds complete and full. The picking guitarist usually plays lines, rhythms, or chords separately, but rarely all three at once. Through slow and diligent practice, the student will be able to develop the pick control that will give the impression that there is a melody, bass line, and chords going on simultaneously. Thus, we have solo plectrum guitar pieces that are purposeful, sound full and atmospheric, and are fun to play.

–Allan Jaffe

CONTENTS

THE CHASE

TRACK 1

By Allan Jaffe

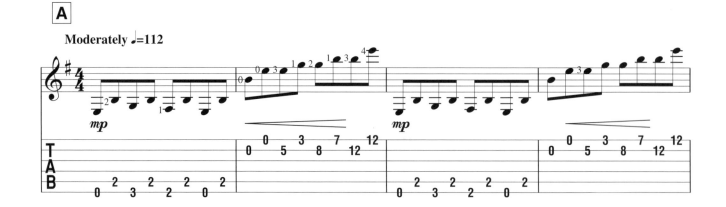

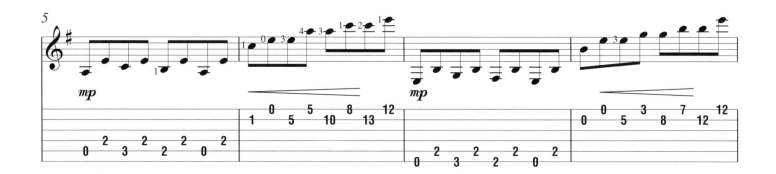

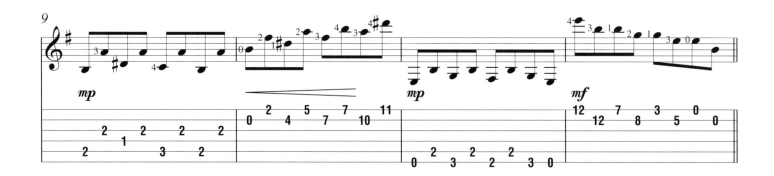

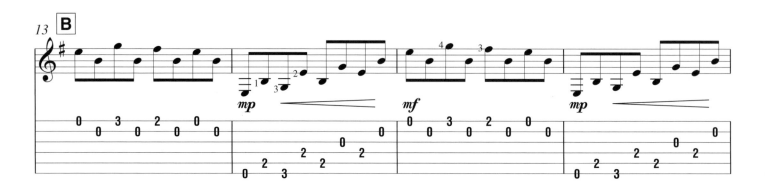

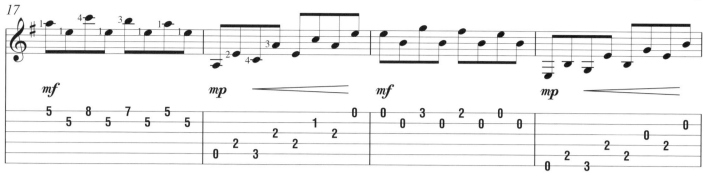

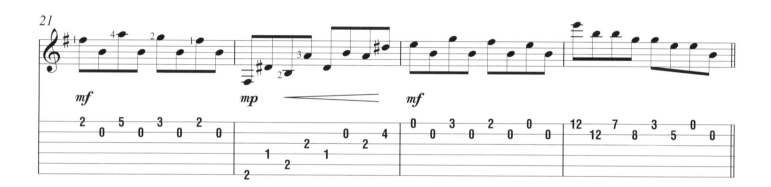

6

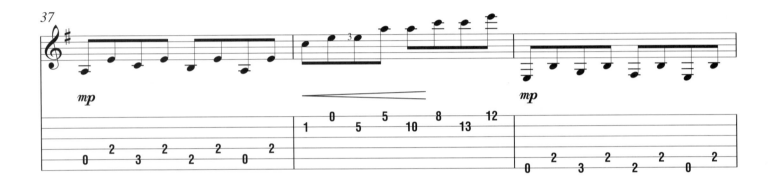

THE GUMSHOE'S SMOOTH MOVE

By Allan Jaffe

TRACK 6

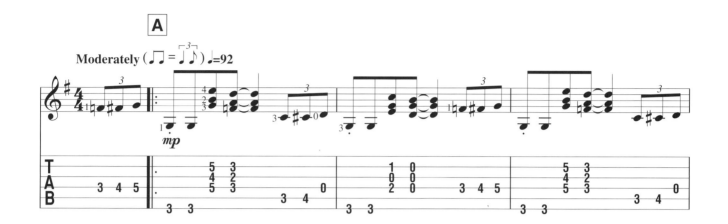

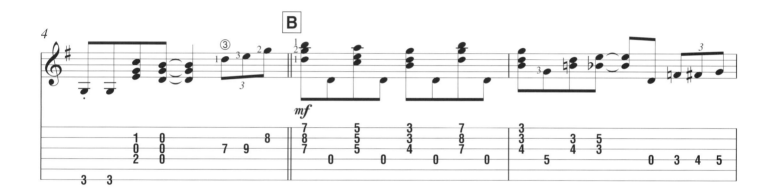

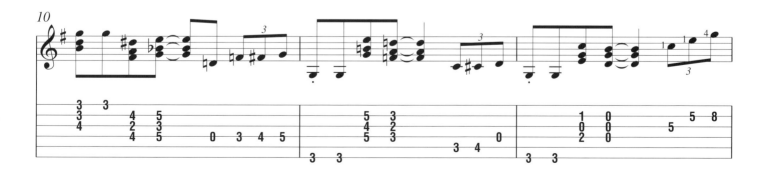

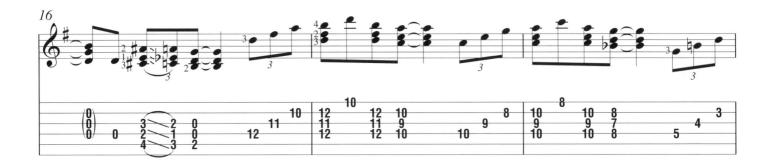

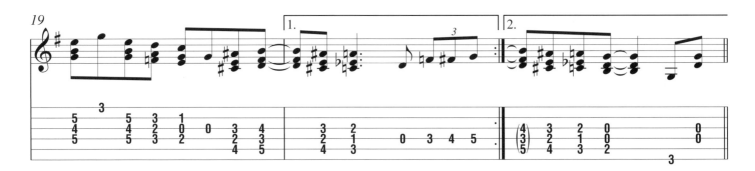

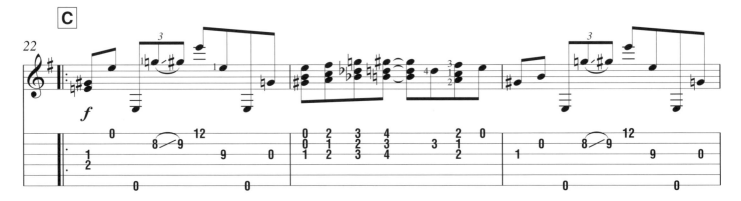

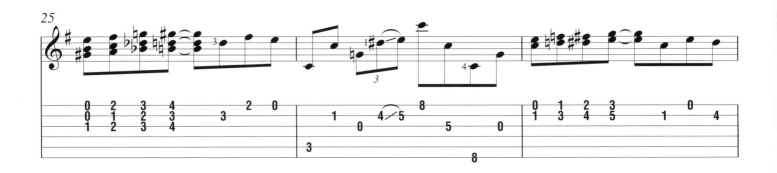

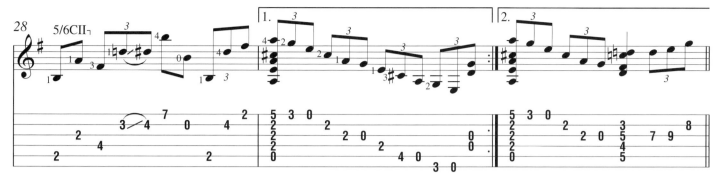

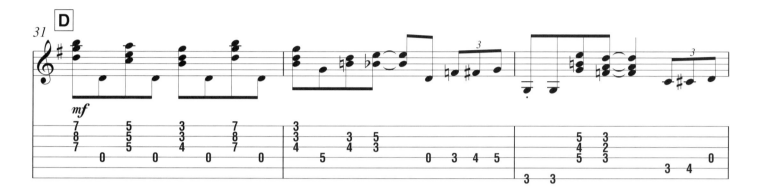

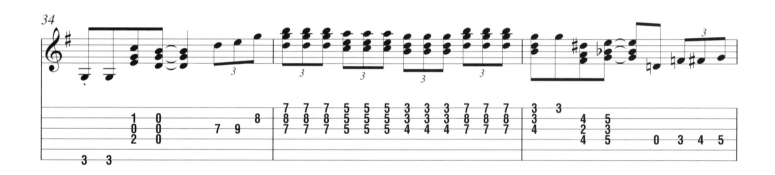

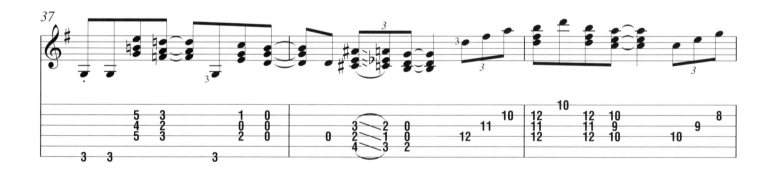

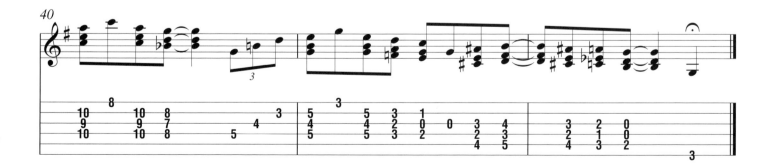

A DAUNTING HAUNTING

By Allan Jaffe

TRACK 2

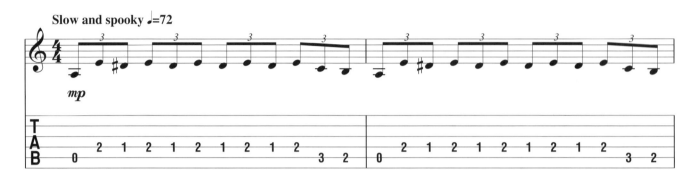

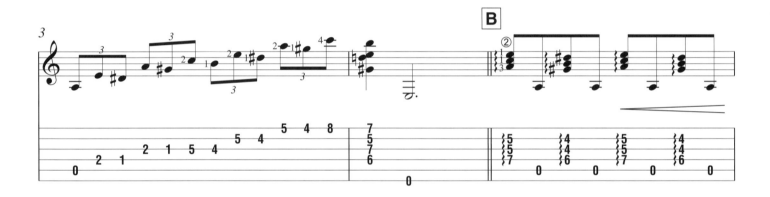

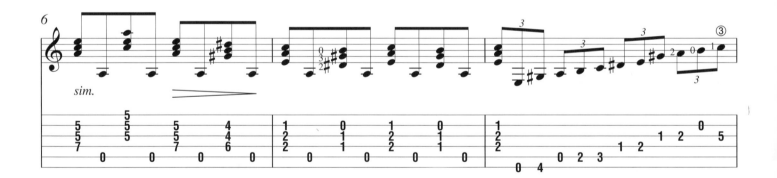

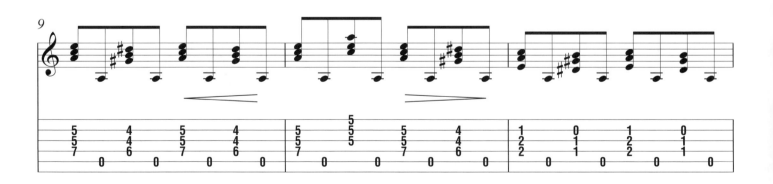

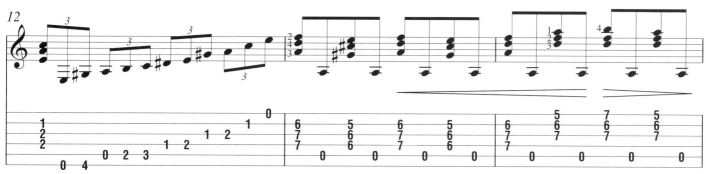

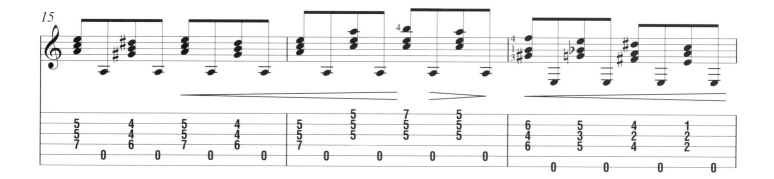

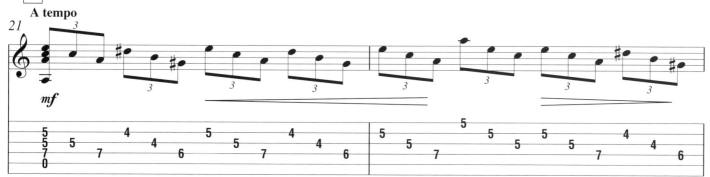

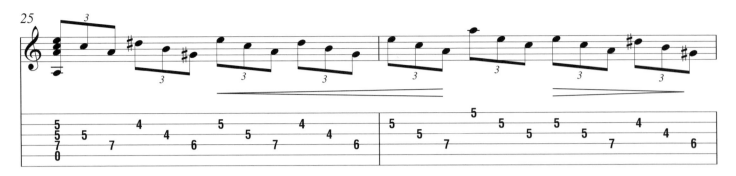

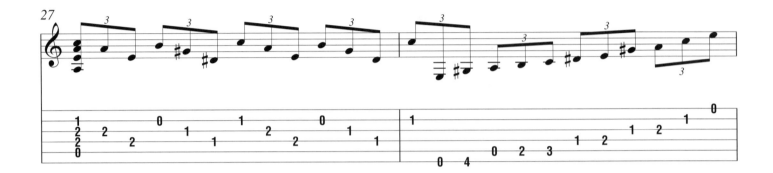

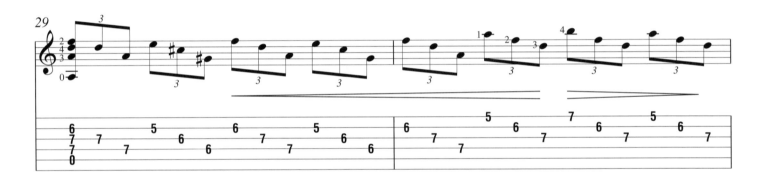

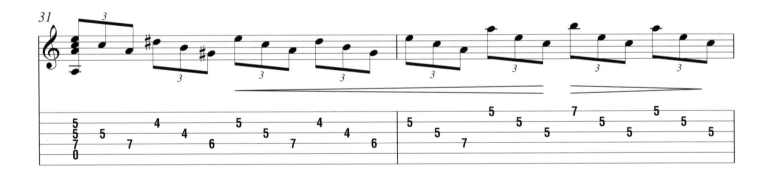

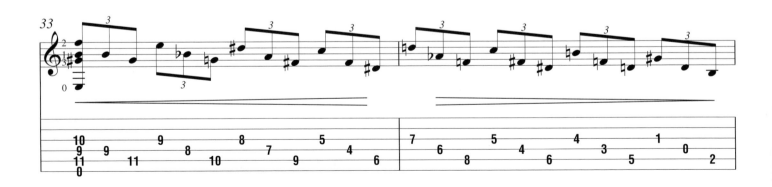

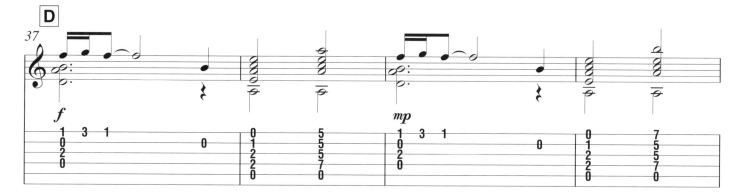

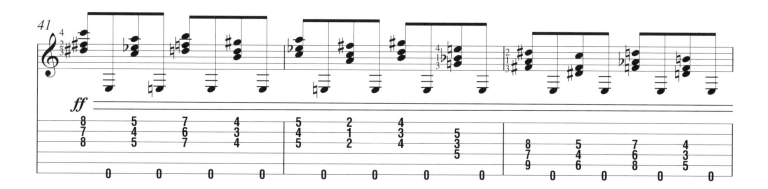

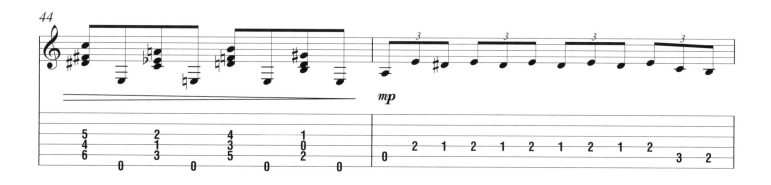

THE DISAPPEARING GUESTS

By Allan Jaffe

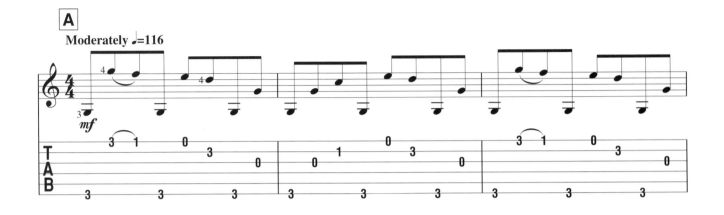

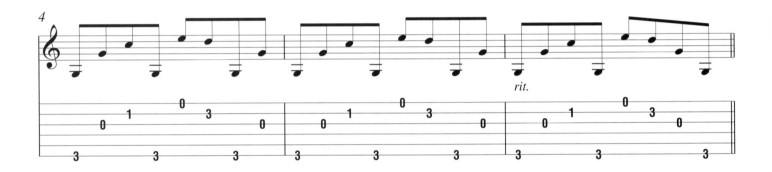

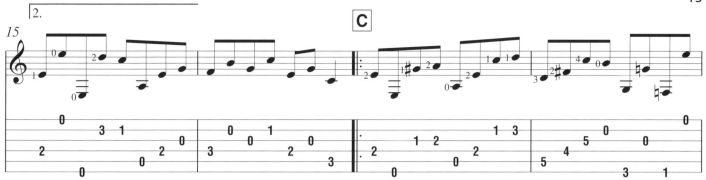

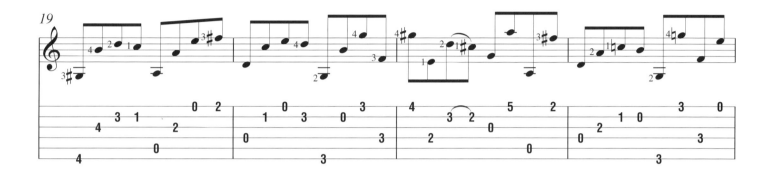

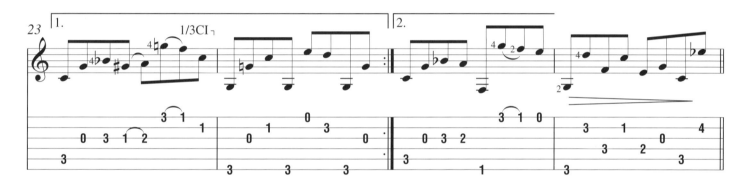

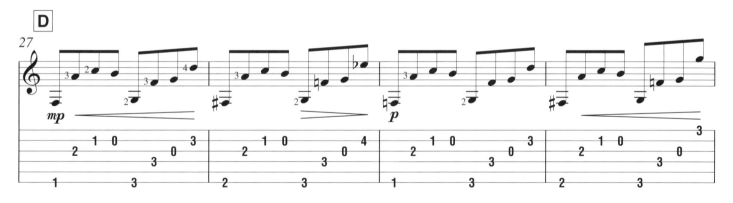

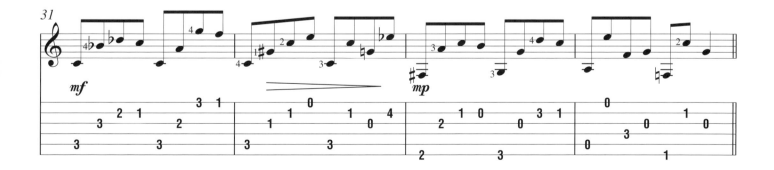

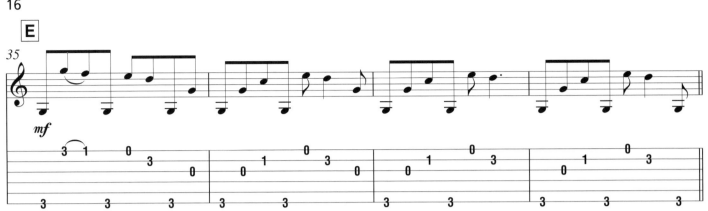

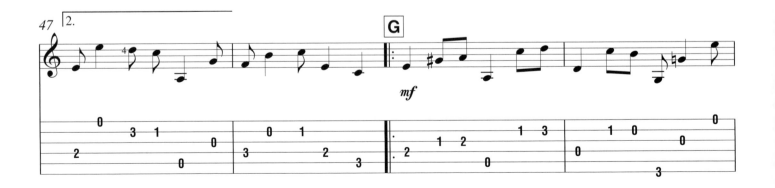

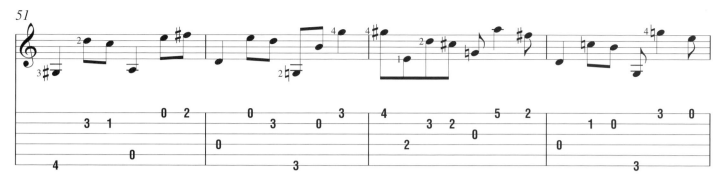

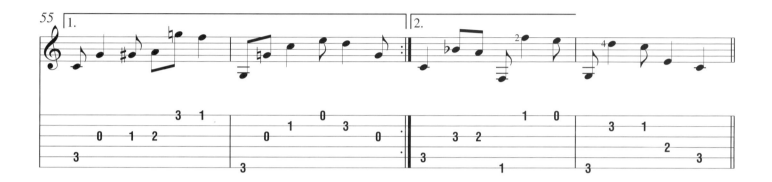

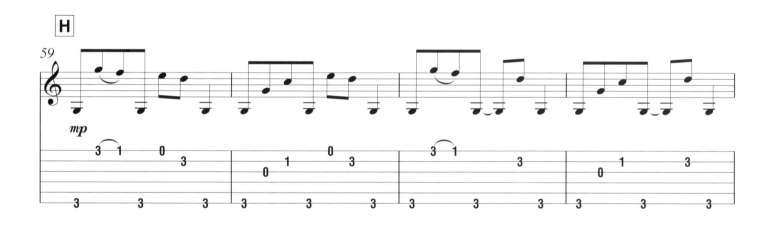

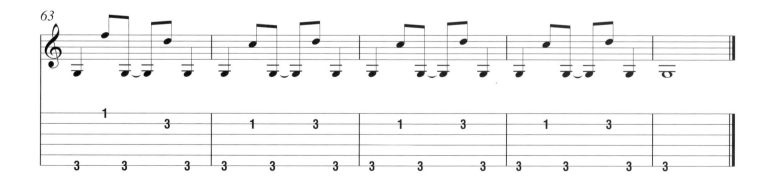

THE GALLOPING NIGHTMARE

By Allan Jaffe

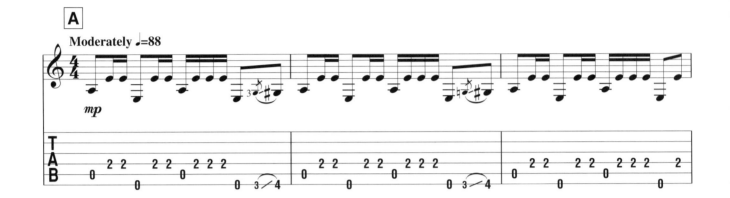

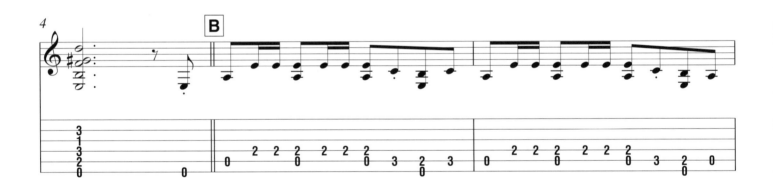

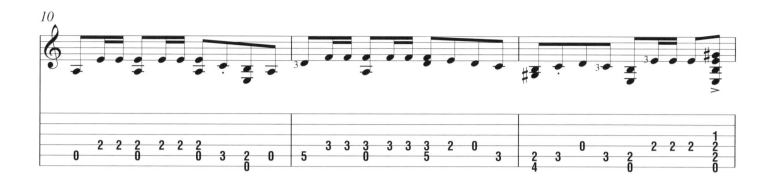

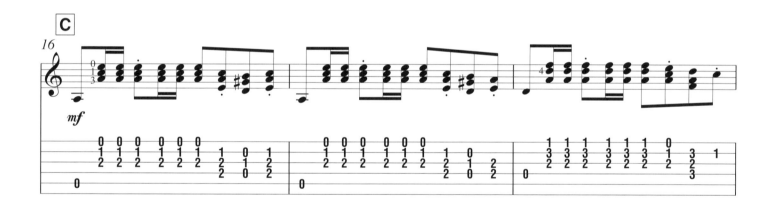

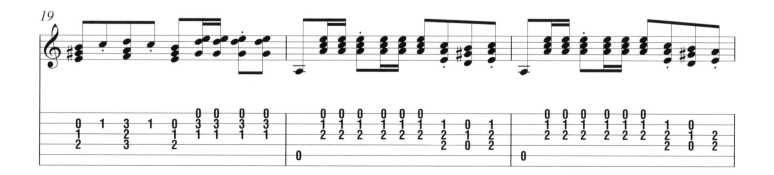

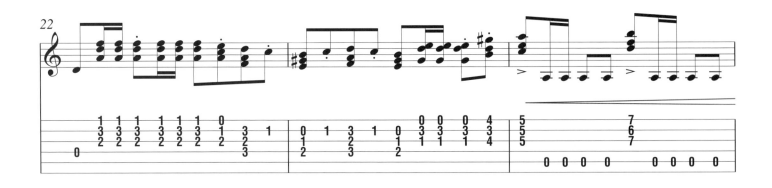

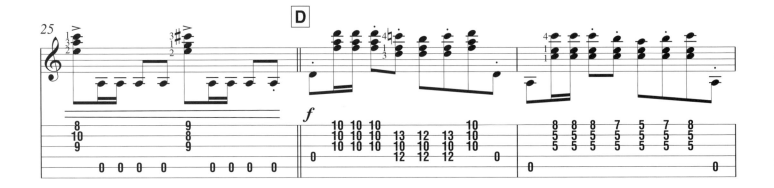

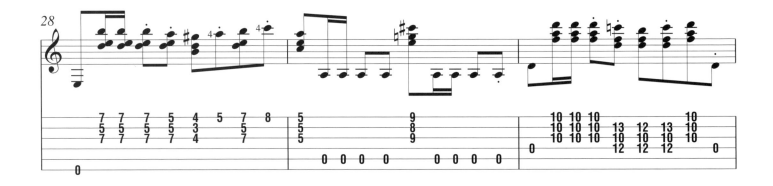

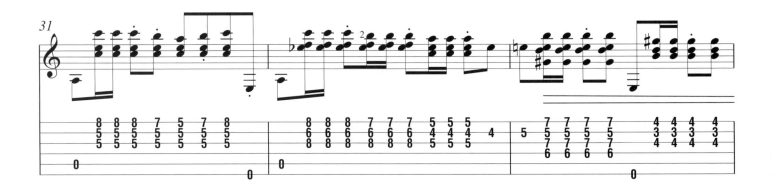

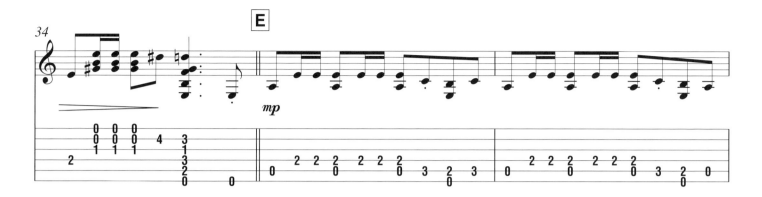

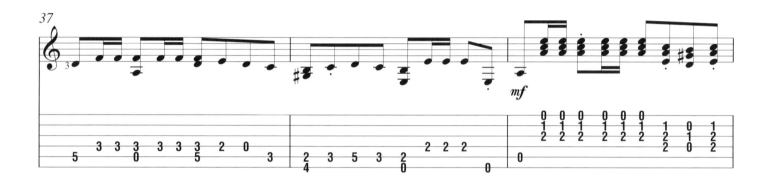

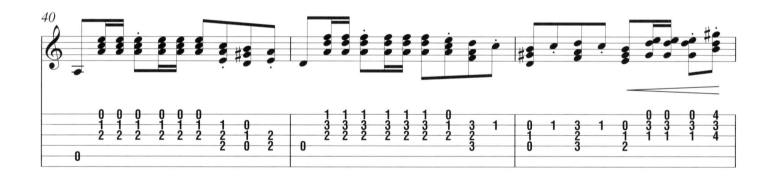

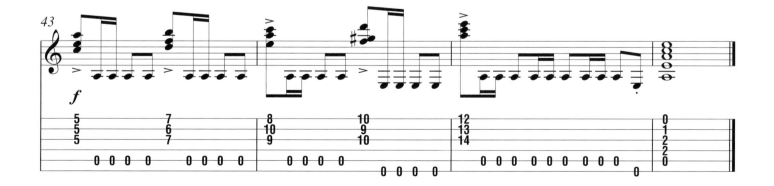

TRACK 5

GUITAR NOIR
By Allan Jaffe

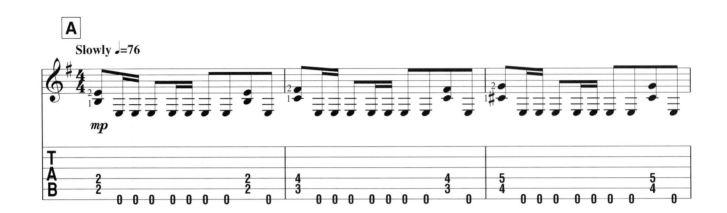

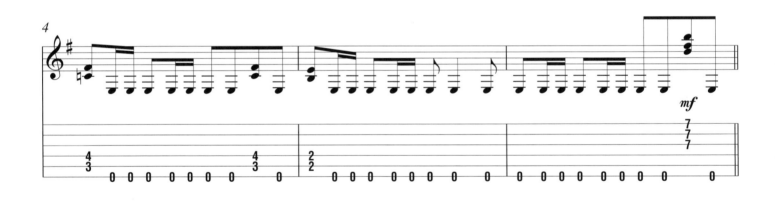

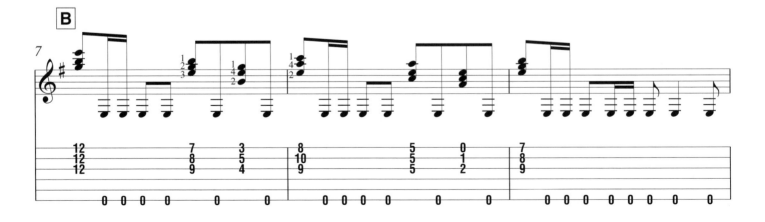

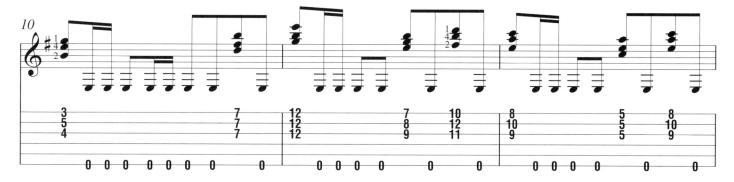

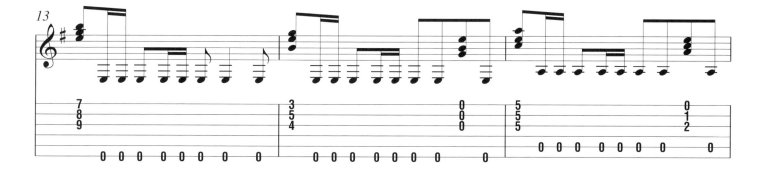

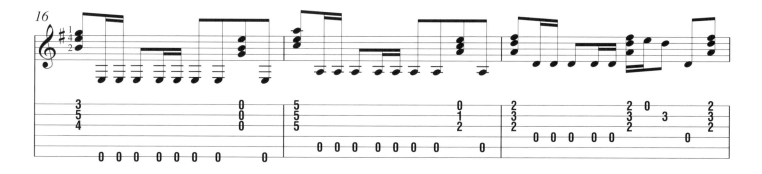

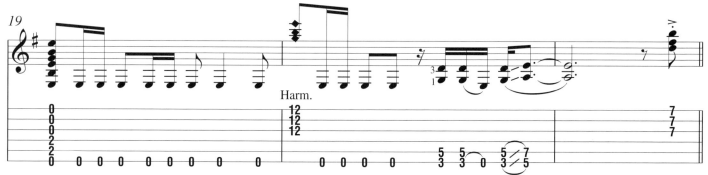

C

More aggressive and rhythmic

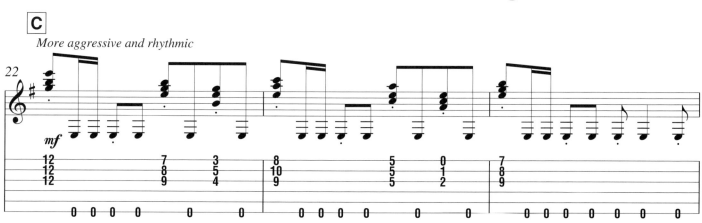

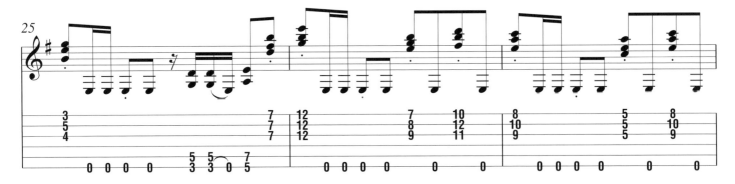

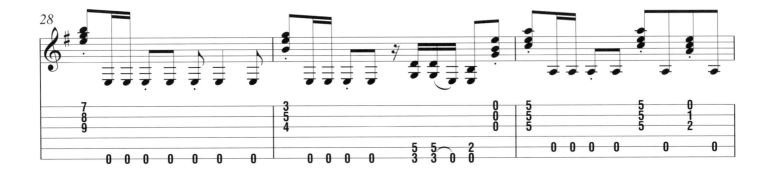

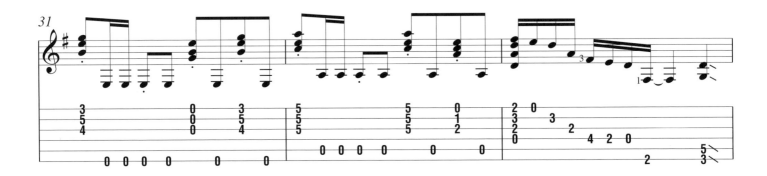

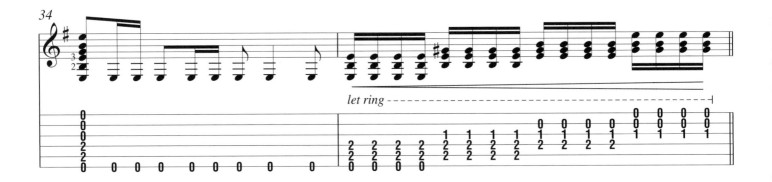

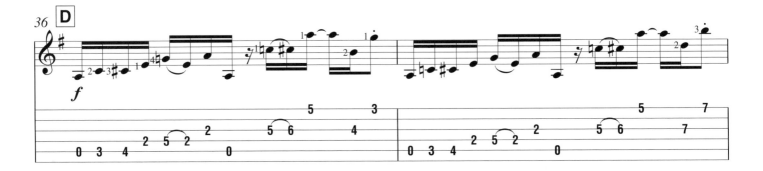

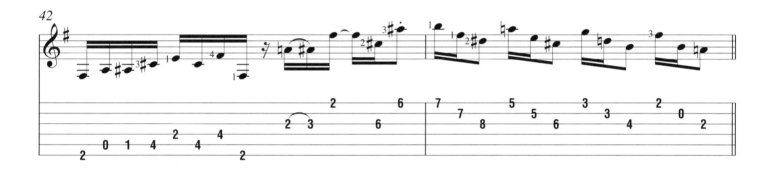

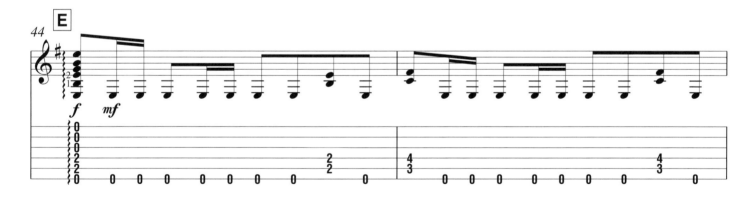

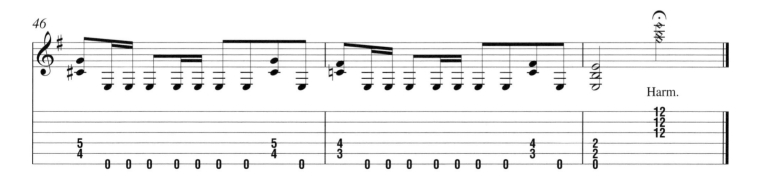

TRACK 7

MYSTERIOSO
By Allan Jaffe

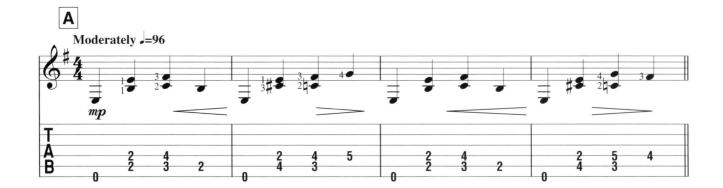

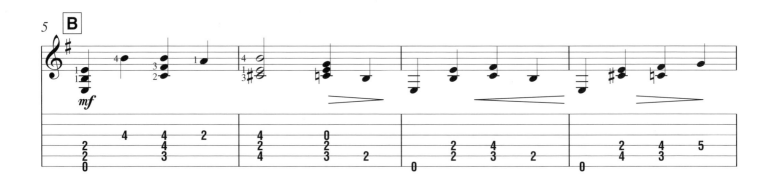

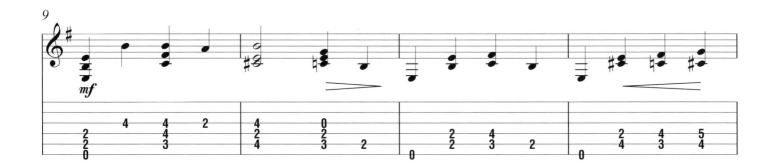

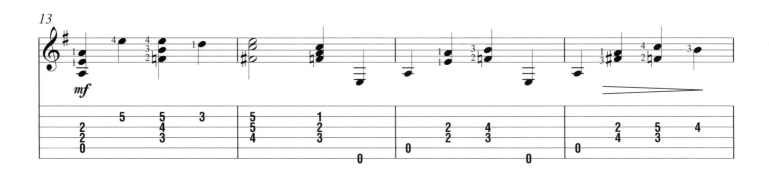

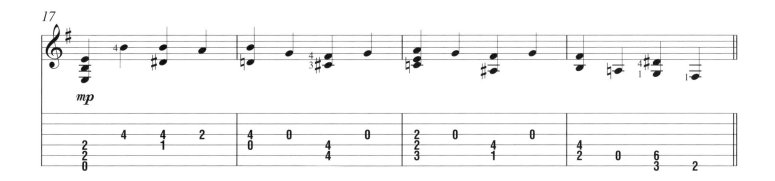

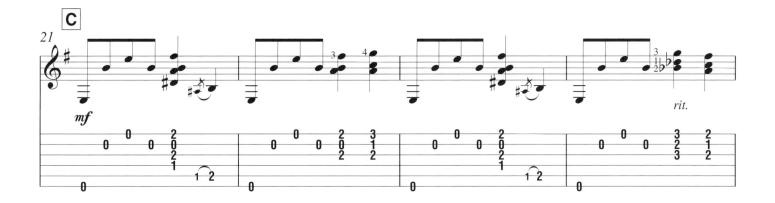

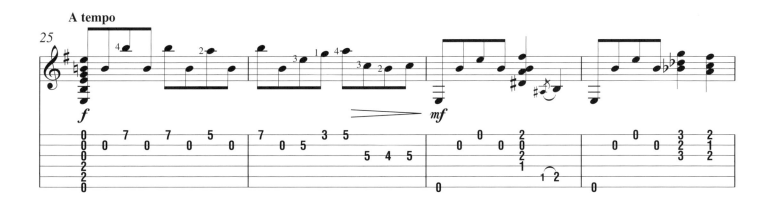

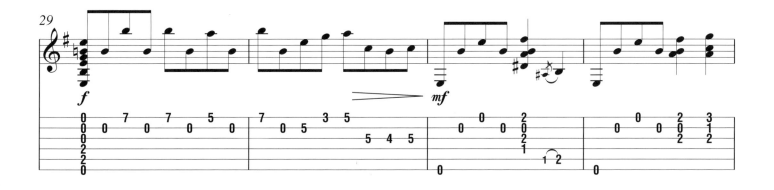

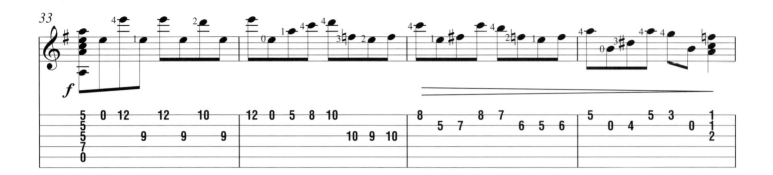

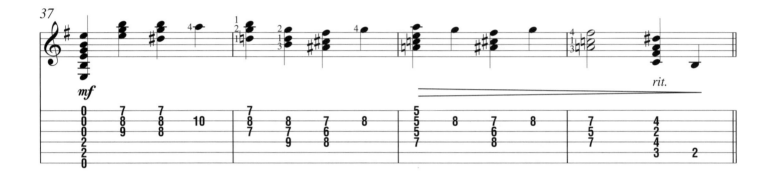

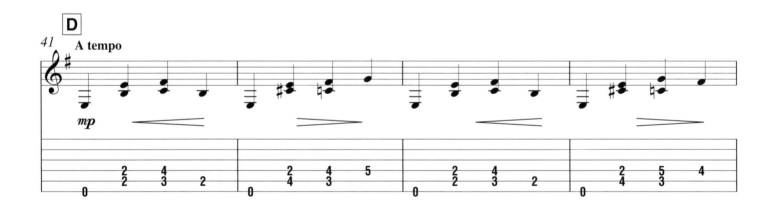

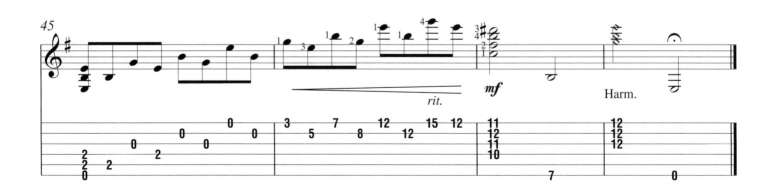

THE PLOT THICKENS

By Allan Jaffe

TRACK 8

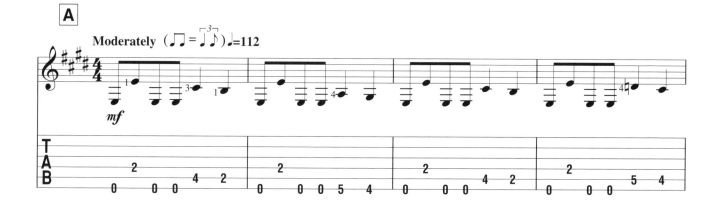

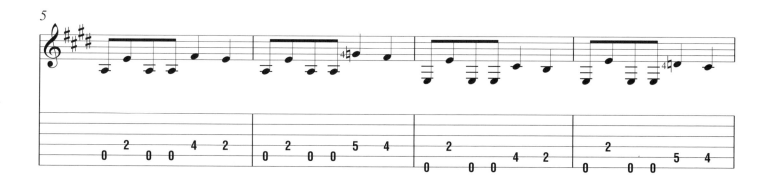

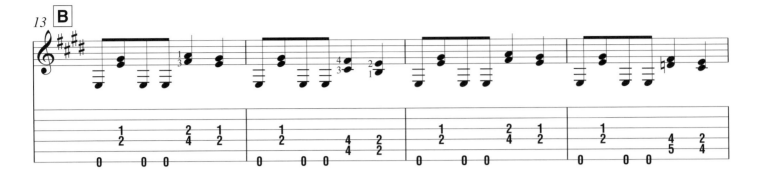

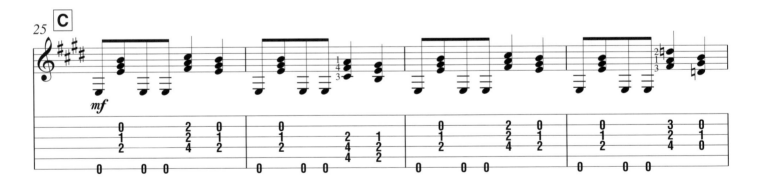

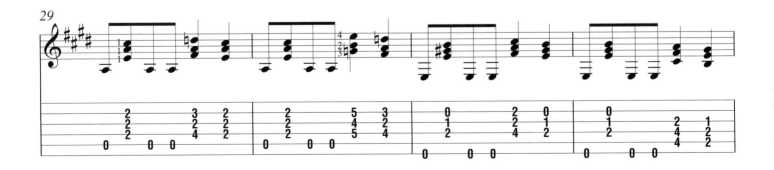

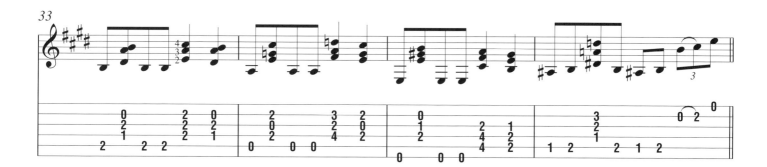

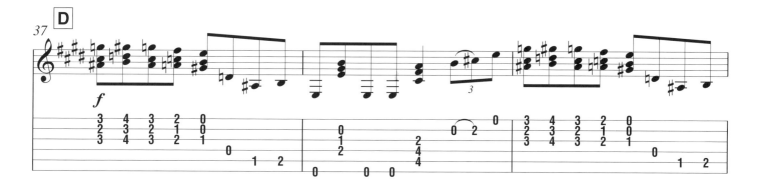

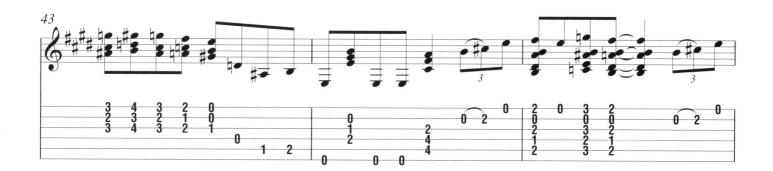

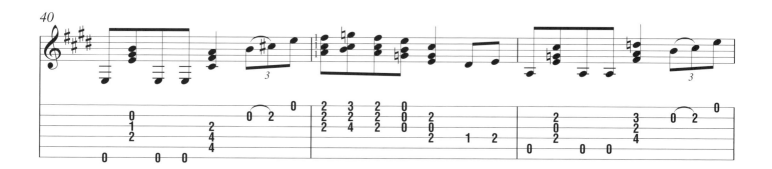

TRACK 9

THE SECRET PANEL

By Allan Jaffe

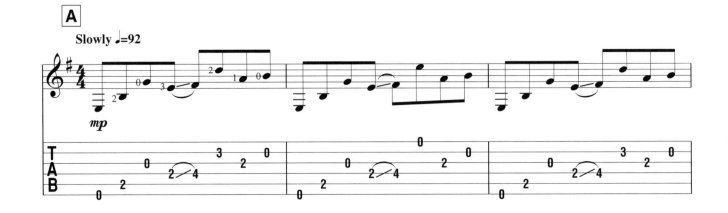

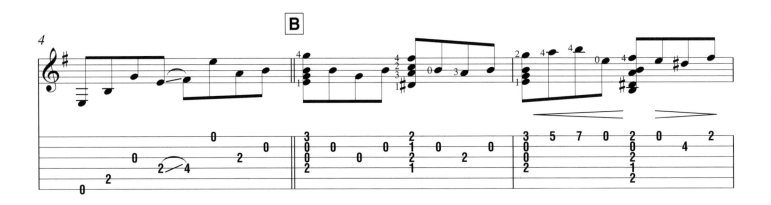

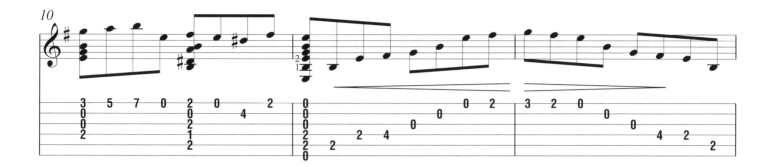

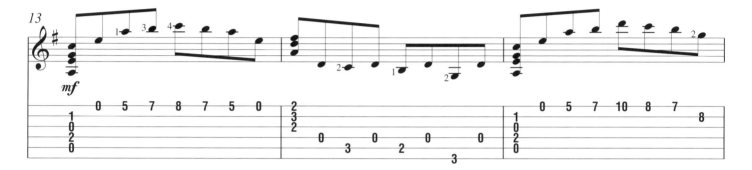

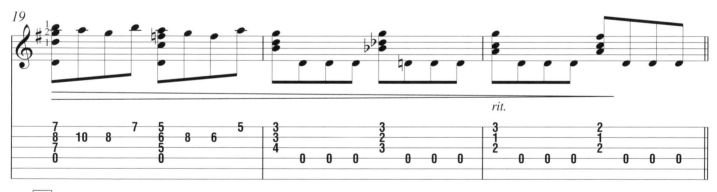

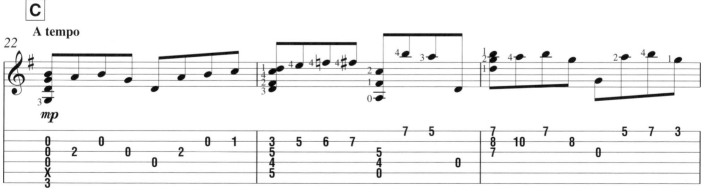

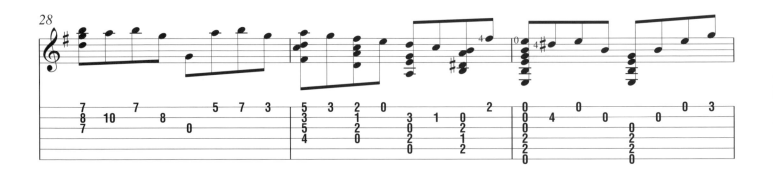

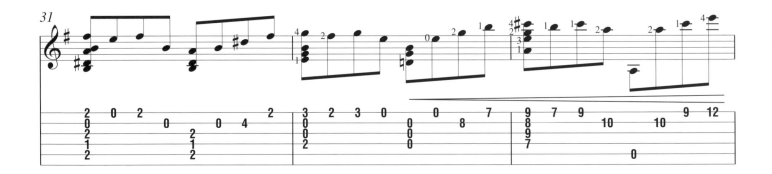

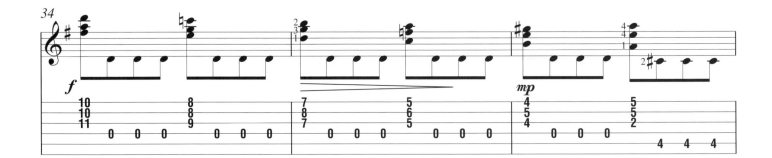

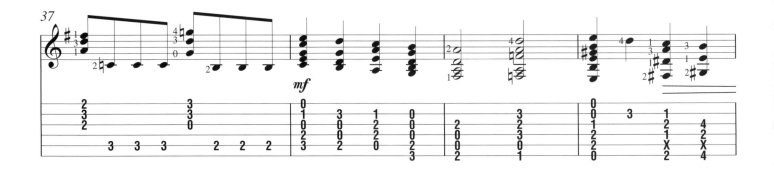

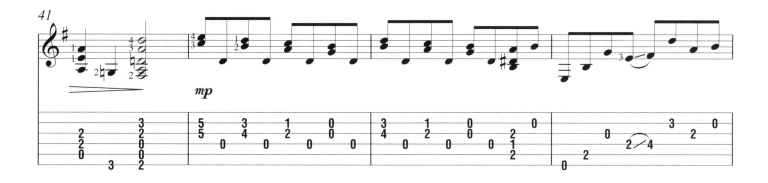

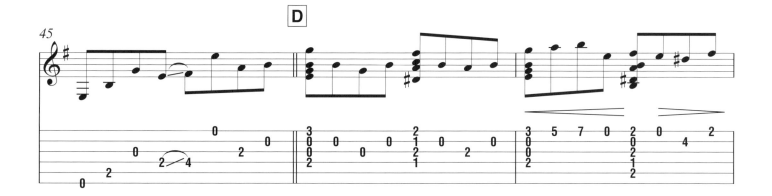

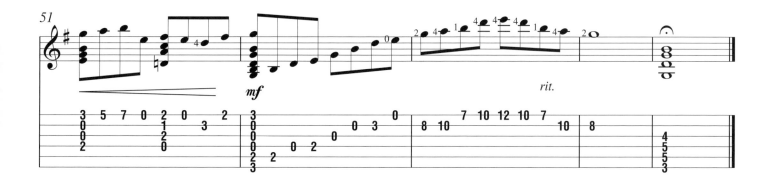

SKELETON DANCE

By Allan Jaffe

TRACK 10

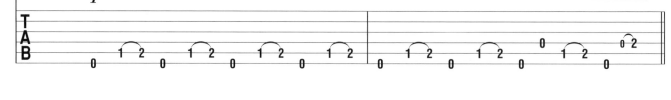

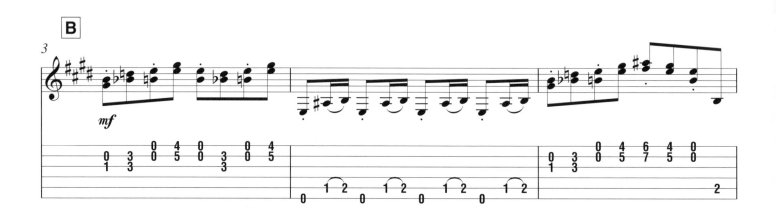

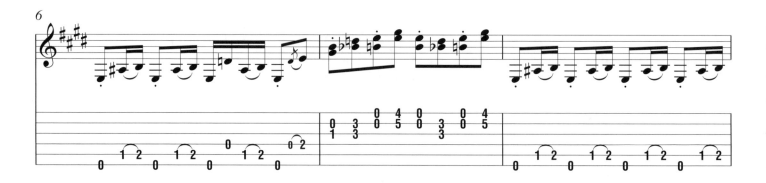

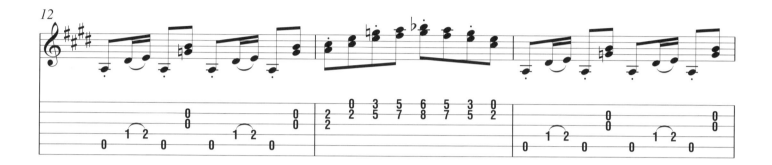

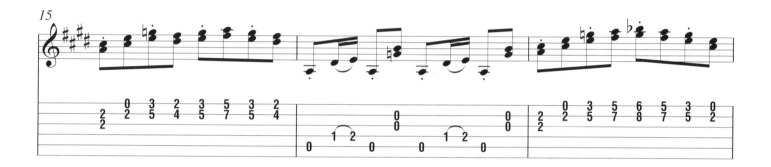

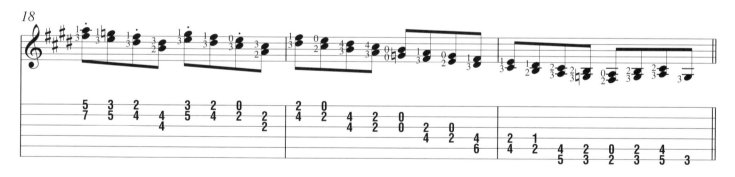

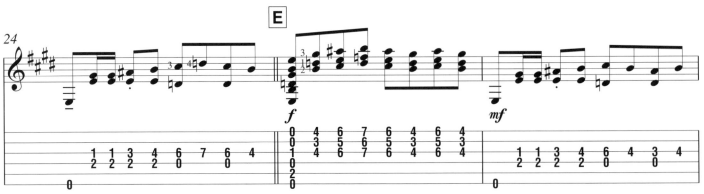

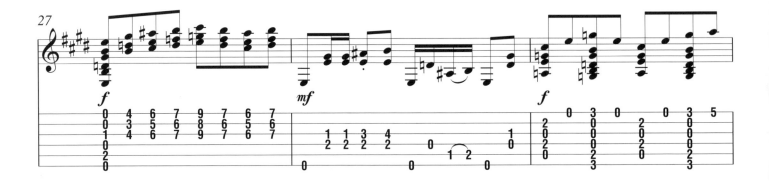

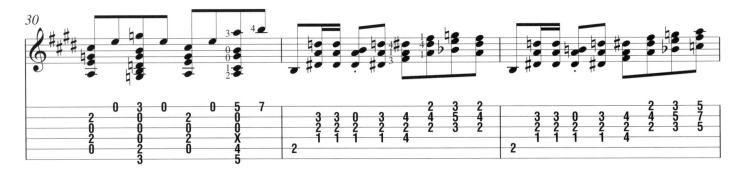

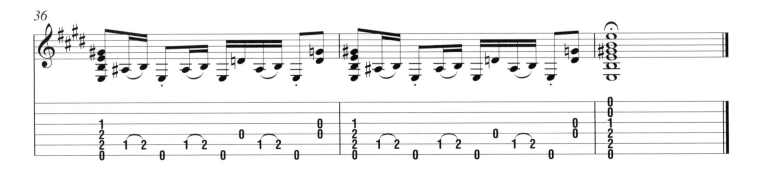

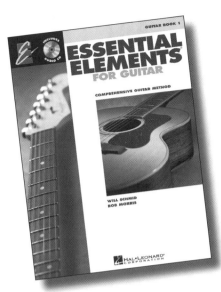

ESSENTIAL ELEMENTS FOR GUITAR, BOOK 1
Comprehensive Guitar Method
by Will Schmid and Bob Morris

Take your guitar teaching to a new level! Hal Leonard's top-selling comprehensive method for band and strings is now also available for guitar. With the time-tested classroom teaching methods of Will Schmid and Bob Morris, popular songs in a variety of styles, and quality demonstration and backing tracks on the accompanying CD, *Essential Elements for Guitar* is sure to become a staple of guitar teachers' instruction – and get beginning guitar students off to a great start.

This method has been designed to meet the National Standards for Music Education, with features such as cross-curricular activities, quizzes, multicultural songs, basic improvisation and more. Concepts covered in Book 1 include: getting started; basic music theory; guitar chords; notes on each string; music history; ensemble playing; performance spotlights; and much more!

Songs used in Book 1 include such hits as: Dust in the Wind • Eleanor Rigby • Every Breath You Take • Hey Jude • Hound Dog • Let It Be • Ode to Joy • Rock Around the Clock • Stand by Me • Surfin' USA • Sweet Home Chicago • This Land Is Your Land • You Really Got Me • and more!

00862639 Book/CD Pack..$17.95

Essential Elements Guitar Ensembles

The songs in Hal Leonard's Essential Elements Guitar Ensemble series are playable by multiple guitars. Each arrangement features the melody (lead), a harmony part, and a bass line. Chord symbols are also provided if you wish to add a rhythm part. For groups with more than three or four guitars, the parts may be doubled. Play all of the parts together, or record some of the parts and play the remaining part along with your recording. All of the songs are printed on two facing pages; no page turns are required. This series is perfect for classroom guitar ensembles or other group guitar settings.

CHRISTMAS SONGS
15 Holiday Hits Arranged for Three or More Guitarists

Songs include: Blue Christmas • The Christmas Song • Christmas Time Is Here • Do You Hear What I Hear • Frosty the Snow Man • Here Comes Santa Claus (Right Down Santa Claus Lane) • A Holly Jolly Christmas • I'll Be Home for Christmas • Jingle-Bell Rock • Let It Snow! Let It Snow! Let It Snow! • My Favorite Things • Rockin' Around the Christmas Tree • Rudolph the Red-Nosed Reindeer • Santa Claus Is Comin' to Town • Silver Bells.

00001136..$9.95

POP HITS
15 Pop Hits Arranged for Three or More Guitarists

Songs include: Best of My Love • Brown Eyed Girl • Dreams • Dust in the Wind • Every Breath You Take • I Get Around • Imagine • Let It Be • My Cherie Amour • Oh, Pretty Woman • Stand by Me • Still the Same • Wonderful Tonight • Y.M.C.A. • Your Song.

00001128 ....$9.95

Essential Elements Guitar Repertoire Series

Hal Leonard's Essential Elements Guitar Repertoire Series features great original guitar music based on a style or theme that is carefully graded and leveled for easy selection. The songs are presented in standard notation and tablature, and are fully demonstrated on the accompanying CD.

TURBO ROCK
Beginner Intermediate Level
by Mark Huls

Turbo Rock features 10 original songs with power chords and riffs. Includes: Blue Steam • Chain Reaction • Dr. Grind • Drive • Fallout • The Fringe • Live Wire • A Rumble and a Hum • Slow Burn • Turbo Rock.

00001076 Book/CD Pack....................................$9.95

BLUES CRUISE
Mid-Intermediate Level
by Dave Rubin

Blues Cruise features 10 original songs with bluesy chords, rhythms, and riffs. Includes: Delta Catfish • Detroit Boogie • Hill Country Stomp • Houston Shuffle • Kansas City Swing • Louisiana Gumbo • Memphis Soul • Southside Man • West Coast Strut • Westside Minor Groove.

00000470 Book/CD Pack....................................$9.95

MYSTERIOSO
Mid-Intermediate Level
by Allan Jaffe

Mysterioso features 10 original songs with spooky melodies and riffs. Includes: The Chase • A Daunting Haunting • The Disappearing Guests • The Galloping Nightmare • Guitar Noir • The Gumshoe's Smooth Move • Mysterioso • The Plot Thickens • The Secret Panel • Skeleton Dance.

00000471 Book/CD Pack....................................$9.95

Essential Elements Guitar Songs

The books in the Essential Elements Guitar Songs series feature popular songs arranged for a specific approach to playing the guitar. Each book/CD pack includes eight great songs.

POWER CHORD ROCK
Mid-Beginner Level

Songs include: All the Small Things • I Love Rock 'N Roll • I Won't Back Down • Mony, Mony • Self Esteem • Smells like Teen Spirit • Talk Dirty to Me • You Really Got Me.

00001139 Book/CD Pack.................................$12.95

OPEN CHORD ROCK
Mid-Beginner Level

Songs include: Brown Eyed Girl • Bye Bye Love • Don't Be Cruel (To a Heart That's True) • Have You Ever Seen the Rain? • Learning to Fly • Love Me Do • Should I Stay or Should I Go • Willie and the Hand Jive.

00001138 Book/CD Pack.................................$12.95

BARRE CHORD ROCK
Late Beginner Level

Songs include: All Along the Watchtower • I Can't Explain • Nowhere Man • (Sittin' On) The Dock of the Bay • Stray Cat Strut • Summer of '69 • Surrender • Wild Thing.

00001137 Book/CD Pack.................................$12.95

FOR MORE INFORMATION,
SEE YOUR LOCAL MUSIC DEALER,
OR WRITE TO:

HAL•LEONARD® CORPORATION
7777 W. BLUEMOUND RD. P.O. BOX 13819
MILWAUKEE, WISCONSIN 53213

Prices, contents, and availability subject to change without notice.